Postcards to Myself

by Nina Freedlander Gibans

Postcards to Myself

by Nina Freedlander Gibans

Copyright © 2022

Cover Design by Jared Bendis

ISBN — 9781626132566

Library of Congress Control Number - 2022942732

Published by ATBOSH Media ltd.

Cleveland, Ohio, USA

www.atbosh.com

Table of Contents

Postcards 10

Paintings and Postcards

The impressionist paintings identified, have been reproduced on postcards.

Impressionism I 12

Beyond Impressionism
Butterflies 13

Impressionism II 14

> *Portrait of Dora Wheeler, 1882–83. William Merritt Chase (American, 1849-1916). Oil on canvas. The Cleveland Museum of Art, Gift of Mrs. Boudinot Keith in memory of Mr. and Mrs. J. H. Wade 1921.1239*

Beyond Impressionism
Reunion 16

Impressionism III 18

> *View of Bordeaux, from the Quai des Chartrons, 1874. Eugène Boudin (French, 1824-1898). Oil on fabric. The Cleveland Museum of Art, John L. Severance Fund and Gift of Mrs. Dudley S. Blossom, Jr. 1986.73*

Beyond Impressionism
On the Shore 20

Impressionism IV 21

> *Dancers, c. 1896. Edgar Degas (French, 1834-1917). Pastel with charcoal on tracing paper mounted on paper and backed with gray board. The Cleveland Museum of Art, Gift of Mr. and Mrs. J. H. Wade 1916.1043*

Beyond Impressionism
Degas Today 23

Impressionism V 24

> *Fifth Avenue, 1919. Childe Hassam (American, 1859-1935). Oil on canvas. The Cleveland Museum of Art, Anonymous Gift 1952.539*

Fifth Avenue Nocturne, c. 1895. Childe Hassam (American, 1859-1935). Oil on canvas. The Cleveland Museum of Art, Anonymous Gift 1952.538

Beyond Impressionism
Beneath the Brick 27

Impressionism VI 28

Sunny Autumn Day, 1892. George Inness (American, 1825-1894). Oil on canvas. The Cleveland Museum of Art, Anonymous Gift 1956.578

Beyond Impressionism
Oregon Truck 30

Impressionism VII 32

The Red Kerchief, c. 1868–73. Claude Monet (French, 1840-1926). Oil on fabric. The Cleveland Museum of Art, Bequest of Leonard C. Hanna, Jr. 1958.39

Beyond Impressionism
My Day Needs Red 34

Impressionism VIII 36

> *Spring Flowers, 1864. Claude Monet (French, 1840-1926). Oil on fabric. The Cleveland Museum of Art, Gift of the Hanna Fund 1953.155*

> *Water Lilies (Agapanthus), c. 1915–26. Claude Monet (French, 1840-1926). Oil on canvas. The Cleveland Museum of Art, John L. Severance Fund and an anonymous gift 1960.81*

Beyond Impressionism
Gardens and Gardeners 40

Impressionism IX 43

> *Bathers Playing with a Crab, c. 1897. Pierre-Auguste Renoir (French, 1841-1919). Oil on fabric. The Cleveland Museum of Art, Purchase from the J. H. Wade Fund 1939.269*

Beyond Impressionism
Grace in the City 45

Impressionism X 46

> *Edge of the Woods Near L'Hermitage, Pontoise, 1879. Camille Pissarro (French, 1830-1903). Oil on fabric. The Cleveland Museum of Art, Gift of the Hanna Fund 1951.356*

Beyond Impressionism
New Hampshire Hill 48

Beyond Impressionism
At the Museum 54

Moving On

Maillart 58

Pandora in a Box 59

Yesterday's Tomorrow 60

Tomorrow Today 61

Counting Cars 62

Afternoon Rises 64

Still Lives

Twists of Wind — 67

Flowers Float — 68

Heather on the Table — 69

Warm words and a Spring Smile — 70

Mud and Matter — 71

This Sunset — 72

A Minor Mood — 73

Summer Months — 74

Finally it's Evening — 77

Memory - A Community of Poets — 78

Fifty Daughters — 79

Agora — 92

Memory — 94

Dear Emily — 95

List of Paintings — 99

About the Author — 102

Postcards

Send postcards.

Give me 20 cents

for truth

friends

who play my mind today

test my mood

guess my thoughts

make me remember

stop

I look now and again

between yesterday's papers

in the drawer of places, times and stories.

Paintings and Postcards

The impressionist paintings, owned by the Cleveland Museum of Art, have been reproduced on postcards.

Impressionism I

I carry the Impressionists around

in my pocket

postcards to my friends; short sentences

my hieroglyphic.

I mail pictures of seas

water nice blue and freckled with sun

(better than the darker troubling ocean.)

I send messages

of hope, laughing.

Carrying these around

I can find friends easily.

Beyond Impressionism
Butterflies

We *still* don't get it

Painters who catch a thought

in the middle of a mood

I need new eyes

blinded by white light

drunk on color-- magicians

stirring air and water

mixing it with our eyes

chasing their vision through windows

to gardens or seashores.

City cafes, sitting spaces become stages

I feel at home

mastering

the magic of butterflies

incandescence and fragility.

Impressionism II

I want to sit in my dress

in my blue dress with fur

and look like I can think

deeply. *I have traveled;*

yellow patterns, Chinese birds, orange butterflies;

yellow flowers only start with daffodils.

She looks at me and knows I know

the unravel of her day but she'd never tell me outright.

                        Traveling light I dress in jeans
                        hoping no one will see me
                        without a handkerchief
                        ladies with blue dresses
                        edged in fur
                        always remembered.
                        she would understand

                        the pants. We are friends.

Portrait of Dora Wheeler, 1882–83. William Merritt Chase (American, 1849-1916). Oil on canvas. The Cleveland Museum of Art, Gift of Mrs. Boudinot Keith in memory of Mr. and Mrs. J. H. Wade 1921.1239

Beyond Impressionism
Reunion

My rearview mirror, memories

brought up to date

after all the years of peripheral vision.

Driving by the dance hall of my youth, I dance again.

I am having a reunion with myself.

I look around for familiar faces,

places to start.

Stories spring memories spin more stories

bring people together with new details.

Glass beads around my neck

reflect stories I want to tell

found in the chandelier of the room

splaying color as tales grow

out of memory and magic.

Flowers on the table, blending bright and subtle

like a smiling friend.

Petals fall like years, one by one.

Through the rearview mirror, street theatre triggers

my part, pressing my script into play.

Lines written just for me

whispered from the wings if I should falter

in this third act

peopled by a cast of friends (from act one and two)

finding their way through dialogue remembered

threads loose, tied, or knotted.

"This is me," I say--Is that a good beginning?

I never could snap my fingers smartly or do small talk.

I will learn now.

Impressionism III

Harbor boats; soldiers of the water
mast sentinels
reflected on the surface
sitting in their own shadows.
rowboats lacing their way to safety
cast an invisible net, settle
bow to bow, and lay like fish
along the shoreline
at the end of day.

                Barges in other rivers
                long and leaden, shift hard
                barely move
                water workhorses

        loaded, weighted, stopped
            dead in sand.

The afternoon stops here;

and slips onto the surface

These days do not move

Boats left for tomorrow

when the sun comes around the cove.

View of Bordeaux, from the Quai des Chartrons, 1874. Eugène Boudin (French, 1824-1898). Oil on fabric. The Cleveland Museum of Art, John L. Severance Fund and Gift of Mrs. Dudley S. Blossom, Jr. 1986.73

Beyond Impressionism
On the Shore

By the lake grounds

Parched this summer to the stubble

Chairs dig in for the duration

webbed strong and rusty, tubular.

Motors, mowers

Branching shadows arch small groups of returning people,

Sitting on dark brown patches in the grass.

Small boats with gulls.

Are they behind or ahead

the stream of summer sound?

Impressionism IV

Dancers resting

or rehearsing

stretching arms

move

in lines or angles

green tulle and yellow grasses

dress the trees

Dancers, c. 1896. Edgar Degas (French, 1834-1917). Pastel with charcoal on tracing paper mounted on paper and backed with gray board. The Cleveland Museum of Art, Gift of Mr. and Mrs. J. H. Wade 1916.1043

Beyond Impressionism
Degas Today

How would Degas

find

        Pilobolus, Da Noise and Tharp

        dressed loose, running free

in the wings

redefining dance

        line and shape

        charging angles, moving round

        chasing green pastels

behind stage?

Impressionism V

Blue Fifth Avenue cast in its own

five o'clock shadow

traffic just before evening

sets a stillness

street quiet

Only enough energy to play patterns

among people and buggies and buildings

vying for attention.

Night is somber

gaslights—street change,

face mirrors on the sidewalk

figures distanced by mood.

Fifth Avenue, 1919. Childe Hassam (American, 1859-1935). Oil on canvas. The Cleveland Museum of Art, Anonymous Gift 1952.539

Fifth Avenue Nocturne, c. 1895. Childe Hassam (American, 1859-1935). Oil on canvas. The Cleveland Museum of Art, Anonymous Gift 1952.538

Beyond Impressionism
Beneath the Brick

In the thigh of the road beneath the stubble of the stones

that lined the edge,

beneath the brick top surface,

lies a history.

Storekeepers sweep the top;

Dirt slides through to the past.

Six solid city streets, packed

with stores and homes, one gas station.

Baking and eating, families keep secret recipes

fresh for next generations.

Impressionism VI

Falls are different when all the colors are
in balance.
I try to guess if it will be that way this year
In years without reds *(It's the moisture, they say)*
I look to see how many maples I can find.
Was the best '92 or '95
Like a full red wine I can see
and taste the color caught in the sun
leaves hovering like a gold and red umbrella
and a fine label.

Sunny Autumn Day, 1892. George Inness (American, 1825-1894). Oil on canvas. The Cleveland Museum of Art, Anonymous Gift 1956.578

Beyond Impressionism
Oregon Truck

Oregon truck, what have you got

Behind the cab, hiding from my view

Across the bridge

Around the bend?

Crowding the land, three rivers hug the earth,

river salmon caught upstream

lazy living, fishing on the front porch of a houseboat

to catch the early edge of sun, salmon-pink,

reflected in the ripples

running side-by-side with logs and fish,

channeled like swimmer's racing routes.

Peach trees' winter pink-bark feather the fields;

the language of the land:

mimosa leaves, squash specialties, earth cupping seed

knoll-high mounds, hay lay anew

waiting for earth blossoms.

Oregon truck, what have you got for me

Behind the cab hidden from my view?

Across the bridge

Beyond the bend?

Impressionism VII

Monet's flame cape

in the fleet moment

of the front window

catches the gray day off guard.

grays his hunger, pushing

into greens, and whites,

and black.

He will never tell us what she looked like

that day in her cape.

He forgets that she is his wife

The Red Kerchief, c. 1868–73. Claude Monet (French, 1840-1926). Oil on fabric. The Cleveland Museum of Art, Bequest of Leonard C. Hanna, Jr. 1958.39

Beyond Impressionism
My Day Needs Red

In the morning
I catch myself in our garden
before I know, for sure, shapes and colors
and how they will *really* look
when they are rooted, rained
and sunned.

                                                                 In the city
moving stairs go nowhere
rings and buzzers,
nonsense
against my day.
I am angry
balancing what I know
and what I talk about
to myself.

My day needs red

the *feel* of cheerful orange

or a square of Hoffman red

between rose red and blood red.

I know my reds and this is how I want them

visiting my mood.

Impressionism VIII

I.
Hyacinths, lilacs, roses in baskets
no waterlilies here
seasides are miles away
no pond
just the spring
from the garden
as fresh today as they were
when they were painted.

II.

On top, under, through

the water

surfaces and depths

caressing every stone, lump of sand, seagrass,

Monet's paintbrush swims

down and around

coloring his seas.

Spring Flowers, 1864. Claude Monet (French, 1840-1926). Oil on fabric. The Cleveland Museum of Art, Gift of the Hanna Fund 1953.155

Water Lilies (Agapanthus), c. 1915–26. Claude Monet (French, 1840-1926). Oil on canvas. The Cleveland Museum of Art, John L. Severance Fund and an anonymous gift 1960.81

Beyond Impressionism
Gardens and Gardeners

Perennials from an old yard,

cuttings to coming years

replanted to space now quarter size

Moonflowers like Jack and the Beanstalk

over careful borders

of parsley, ageratum, begonias.

room for solitude

the heart of mindlessness

hands into moisture, dirt, color--

yellow masts on a lake

sailing day dreams, sunny thoughts

no sequence, no consequence.

watching and remembering

gardens and kitchens, birds spreading seeds

aprons shaking cookie crumbs into the day.

Dried yarrow in the sun room, clumped mustard heads

silver dollars turning in an earthen vessel

or wrapped for giving and sharing.

Colors from childhood--Romania, Austria, England, Ireland

family tradition dahlias, lobelia, blue salvia

histories of tiger lilies, hosta and geranium

remembered reds-countries, places, people

veronica, daisies, inherited jonquils

brought to this garden now.

new gardeners plan edges and groupings,

learn names and traditions

from those who have dug a lifetime.

sharing tomatoes from a basketful

of success, surprise oregano flowers

smelling like fresh Italian sauces.

Prime flowers deep blue dainty phlox plucked secretly

Tucked into an otherwise ordinary day.

Impressionism IX

Who is your muse, 'graces"?

sized between

Botticelli and Rubens

playing against the rock forms

open shells

in sunlight

pearl-white skin glistening

against the sand.

                    They are *all* graceful

                    goddesses

                    Renoir's women mediate

                    form and light

                    the only ones

                    having fun.

Bathers Playing with a Crab, c. 1897. Pierre-Auguste Renoir (French, 1841-1919). Oil on fabric. The Cleveland Museum of Art, Purchase from the J. H. Wade Fund 1939.269

Beyond Impressionism
Grace in the City

Grace in the city.

It's the closest I come to having a Picasso of myself,

the fractured face in my rearview mirror,

a framed. quarter-head, upper forehead

outlined by the street behind.

abstract through sun-lines

changing moment to moment.

time-fractured, sliced

nose and head twisted,

side and front sudden strangers;

I look and know it's me again.

Impressionism X

Green at its densest

I know a path nearby--miles away from France

that I look at

tree for tree, green for green,

leaf and light

Pisarro led me there.

in the cooler summer,

near fall, when the leaves dress

and the goat waits to be tethered, hosed, patted, milked.

Edge of the Woods Near L'Hermitage, Pontoise, 1879. Camille Pissarro (French, 1830-1903). Oil on fabric. The Cleveland Museum of Art, Gift of the Hanna Fund 1951.356

Beyond Impressionism
New Hampshire Hill

I.

It's Spring.

Croc-skinned,

Leading to the mountain

the path between the highway and the hill

weaves a pebble trail years deep with scattered prints.

It is night, no streetlights or porchlights spot the way.

A patchwork of lights line the dark blue nightquilt.

Not one historic thread reflected in a thousand standing rains.

Scatter shots of history; albums in the leaves.

Tracks blend and crunch into the soils of time

sinking pebble by pebble with today's rain; like penpoints.

I thread my step across the piles of dirt besides the shacks;

bone-thin cows, dry-haired dogs, doors on ground, flat

leaving yellow holes in the doorframes.

A single semi-mansion stands, clapboard clean and simple.

Hemmed by a rose garden, nestling bulbs about to sprout

markers for new eyes.

II.

I'm here now; I'm from the city.

I see an Elm tree's sun-stained bark

etched against a sky that's country blue.

A cloud-slit view beyond the path,

Clearer for me than for those who see it every day.

Clearer for me than for the bird stopped in its track

Ear-bent to the earth.

Who has walked this wood? Half-moon shadows in the afternoon

Round the trunk like applique?

Masks of sunlight flirt through leaves.

I can roam farther than the path can lead to other conversations,

other times with ease.

Now, in the sun-slit day spider twigs, bird-feet shaped to weightlessness,

feather my thoughts.

Who has withered or gained strength

from the broad and sweeping volumes of the clouds?

III.

And the trees. Where did a single one stand out

left when the house was built upon the bank?

Who knows the brethren beams

Stalked by winds

Smacked by storms

Leveled in their prime

Chopped and stacked

Wood on wood shifted piece by piece.

I went by the tree when it was tall.

Now it's stacked with dignity

was it a lovers' tree?

Scripts on the bark

Connected family gifts with givers,

carved of self and selves

Connecting spoken phrases and unspoken thoughts

unfinished conversations--

bridging Fridays and Mondays, the child self and present self

spanning Decembers and Januaries, Summer and Winters

one with the present.

IV.

Was it in a dream?

Mind half-opened to the day revisited

Half-open windows; in the cool of the crack

a pleasing storm pummels the night

pokes sound to quiet some decision.

the splattered dream-light

seen through to the half-eye view

No decision in the storm of yellow light

The wood stack and the path are one with the highway and the hill

one with the split-level and high level; the mansion and shattered shack

one with the night and the storm

the tree and the wooden logs

Assemblage of the past

the disassembled years.

One by one, trees fell to the years ahead

Between "Paterson" the man-city, and "Prairyerth" the county, lies the story of a woodland, a piece of land "between the mountain and the road", between the New England frame and the shamble, between the old timer and new timer. The trees cut down, a stack of wood, reconsiders paths to glory, and rumored decisions about this trail of leaves and lives, stilled stories of many generations, of hoofs, and wheels and boots which tracked and traced along the snow or soil. It knows the hunters by their first names called in the wind and the neighborhood chorus of the one time or many-time visitor. It breathes in the sun deeply.

Beyond Impressionism
At the Museum

Yesterday

I got lost, on a two-lane road

when I was supposed to turn on to the four-lanes

to 61. For 11 miles, I shared space with one biker

until he disappeared in the seat of the valley, body hunched

to the physics of the road. I passed him. No cars,

I could wind with the tree-forms in the yellow harvest

brown guideposts where wheat was waiting to be cut.

Today at the museum

Minefield of labels, images stalking the words

I want to talk back to the painting,

It was a purple road, and the biker's cap was yellow.

The meadow a sprinkle of red cayenne on salad greens;

the wheat field was ready. I was a painter

It was our space.

Today in the city

Earth yawning at the new foundation. Whose birthright?

A city's crumbling links to this day

history splayed when the earth was dug

covering the gardens of those who made the city,

the homes no one remembers.

Stories wrap around buildings and people

memories held only in diaries and paintings.

Yesterday

I'm lost on the streetcar going down the hill

with real perspective, orange sun on the window

trees and wires mix for blocks in all directions,

no marked paths, no marked turn; my eyes are the guide

through side streets and some standing houses brick and vines;

peeling chimneys, fading carpets, abandoned rooms

best at sunset in the rosy light.

The land has been flat for so long that

I celebrate survival.

Today I look at paintings, and remember.

Moving On

Maillart

Bridging unknown towns

Pen and ink on deckle-edge

sky-blue.

Breaking age-old silences

etched in mountain rock

Gently mingling memories with mountain lore

Deep secrets.

Maillart built bridges between mountains in Switzerland spanning valleys and cultures never before able to communicate.

Pandora in a Box

The trouble with history is not that we change it
We don't KNOW it!
We throw it away;
papers tossed, dumped
boxed, shelved, labeled, unopened
Careful Pandora
upright please, do not shift contents,
change the verbs or adjectives
the mood, the settings.
Listeners hang on. Three chances,
speak five languages, spell it right,
ask good questions.
original documents
(Plato on Ideas.)
No lingering on facts,
Just memory in shadow.

Yesterday's Tomorrow

Today is yesterday tomorrow
A limb from a tree
we were growing. Broken.
Unless we make connections,
re-grow this limb, swaddle it to
healing.
This day will go unnoticed.

Tomorrow Today

When we reach tomorrow

we will set the table (it will be today)

for a feast to the future.

We will spin our cloth of sun colors

and earth dyes from soils of many countries;

we will listen to many birds

world-wise languages imitate

forest voices never heard;

we will eat alluvial-fruit, desert herb, mountain snow--

tame our taste to new climates.

We will build higher

and go deeper into the earth and sea.

We will gather around a new bonfire

to relive movies, open old boxes, retell stories,

beginning with a favorite and ending with our own.

Counting Cars

We rode by the old house

A child, sitting on a wooden swing

was watching the whole world pass

making up the games I made up when I lived there.

I could tell--counting cars, this time *mine* counted

and *she* could guess where *I* was from and where I might be going.

Porches were for best-friend talk, popsicles;

made-up schemes

shared with friendly cats,

Hopscotch rain or shine,

just far enough beneath the eaves to keep us dry

the rear view mirror caught long shadows

of my favorite tree—tall and wise

so quickly planted to celebrate our moving in.
The dark lines stretching to the iron fencing--
look like giant pick-up-sticks.

Afternoon Rises

Empty streetscapes stalk the city
everywhere.
Will they be filled again
fixed with style,
or be packaged neatly, ribbon-wrapped
delivered,
or, just become?

>one shopkeeper sweeps
>lets the day
>work its way across the shop-front
>scattering debris like sidewalk stories
>swept to the curb
>rolled into dust.

Broken bricks cut the horizon
sharper than glass; cut the city

on the way to the waterfront;

disgorged buildings stumble into view;
hard to look, hard to turn away
Tarp and rags—piled uneven covering
decades of living
stained.

    In a clearing, one old armchair
    tossed, collects stories and dust;
    A mason lathers top edges
    lets afternoon rise over the rim
    rise over dirt and debris,
    Refurnishing.

Still Lives

Twists of Wind

When Spring came

it was like a new idea

surprising me I thought I knew every possibility

I thought I knew every flower, especially white ones

this one opened white and broad

in the vase on the table.

The cup inside

bristles like a small used paint brush

dipped in soft brown ink

ready for delicate lines.

A still life with vase on the dark brown table.

Flowers Float

Flowers float in my head, mindful of color

exactly as they were at 6 am, 10 am, noon.

At 6 pm I closed the screened door and held a pot full of mostly purple.

That was Sunday.

the table top is sprinkled purple, Wednesday, this handful

deep fading to a rose against the wood table brown

in three days aging to another time.

How Victorian. The romantic mauves seem

like an anticipated weekend--a long

3 days in prime patches of sun, catching new energy,

Wilting at the airport on the way home.

Heather on the Table

When night begins

lights hang, a necklace on the city

on a collar of trees.

A montage: the door, white panel, the painting, just the edge,

a jade plant on the ledge just to the graying sky

still smoldering from the sunset

a new triptych of dining room themes

Three parts: the brown long table, woven chairs

and me, writing.

Heather buds drop to decorate the table

for dinner.

Warm words and a Spring Smile

It was supposed to be a warm Spring day

in early May

I drove thirty miles

to see a friend

raindrops traced

uneven streaks on the windshield

clouds hung over

dogwood leaves

lacing out

pink and prime

spreading pattern gently

miles thinned

rain lined

the bottom of the glass

warm words

filled the space between us

Mud and Matter

No shadows, just clear reflection

of mud and matter

etched on waters

only other worlds change;

this for centuries

each new viewer

a first time.

This Sunset

Round and very red the sun moves
straight down the window pane at 8
like a painter brushing red
round shapes; a streak-thin layer of cloud
first holds it up, then dissects it unevenly
until it's silhouetted.
I look down at the buildings
greyed and muted as evening blends into
the night rising charcoal
upstaging lights from cars moving and stopping,
moving and stopping on the street below.

A Minor Mood

A minor mood

reflected

as a pebble tossed into

              water.

lazy circles, slightly wrinkled

become a solid mirror, slowly.

water's slow dance on the surface.

Summer Months

Summer months

burst in upon that short time

we wanted to call Spring--

Interrupting conversations

in the grass trees with noises of the streets

as birds test flight and pickings

cross-hatching overhead

catching seedlings on their tong<u>es?</u>

The windows of the morning

open on the passing coolness of the night

There was Spring.

It was there on new-washed rocks

on new lime greens.

The sun was shy before

this morning

it steals the softness from

the silent slipping Spring.

Hot.

Cars and Dreams

From brick to pebbles and patches

Stories have it

that the man who laid the brick came

to lay a fortune bigger than the brick;

his dream was in the fortune; cars roll over his dream everyday.

Flowers in the yard, story in the vines

trailing tendrils, dense

Dreams hover under eaves, behind the glass door with the lace hanging.

Light finds its way

into the path of the story

The dream was in the light.

Shadows of the morning glory choke the dream.

Wake up; the sun is trying to be bright.

So bold it cannot look you in the eye.

The dream is to look at the sun, squarely.

Whistler's Day

You can't *see* the day,

mist over rooftops

the mood is gray

horizons,

tethered by conditions

humble.

Finally it's Evening

From the north and west

I knew the storm was coming

catching its tale

between noon and All Things Considered. They said I should watch.

If I went south, would it follow?

Like when you're watching the moon

and it's following you?

The clouds tried to gather

at 1 p.m ; sprinkles on the patio

at 3 the sun tried hard

and burst at 5

almost too late to beat dusk.

Memory - A Community of Poets

In 1959, in San Francisco, in the middle of the Beat Era, five un-beat poets met weekly to write together. The following are excerpts from a joint poem written under the supervision of Vincent McHugh who was a friend and colleague of Bennett Cerf, Clifton Fadiman and Allen Ginsberg. In the 1930s, after being editor in chief of the New York office of the Federal Writers Project, he was a staff writer for the New Yorker. I was one of the five poets.

Fifty Daughters

1.
These fifty daughters...
                       and he
went up to it
         black knat
         at the lamp
Ikaros
swirling ladies
you shall find
flaring
     turning
         gyring
            falling
into sea wink
         His coral-fire bed..................

2.

Now at the year's death

                                These deathless

Kourai pentekonta

                        of blameless Nereos

the glitter glass

on black

                        shriek of the seagirls

a pouring swash of dolphins in bright air

----and Nereos, they say

                        couldn't tell one from another:

                            fifty of them

cliffs

        echoing their songs

           yell on yell

    polo-pony

        swerve

    of the dolphins

the whole populous seas

          all heave and sound

    <u>sun</u>

    <u>sun</u>

      and song

3.
Office of the Dead
    forgotten
That they bear
   all heros
   into Hesperides
<u>'In the middle of the ocean</u>
<u>'there shall grow</u>.....
<u>A burning man out of the sun</u>
Timeless
they race
    hull-borrowed trough
mocking at the sail-benders
skating easy on the whale slick
catch prayer-wailing in the storm

from deck-legged masters

sea sea in a boil

a splash of fin half wing

subsiding

in the swell's hollow

4.

So under

      into silence

Barred elbows

Of slow light

      as of a low moon

eyes

      bright in moony shadow

'Green locks of the Nereids...

           Horace

        Streaming

           As in a great wind

Time lost

                    old worlds forgotten

coral fire

gilt with dust

          blood of the Gorgon's head

          cut off by Perseus

these lumps of coral

                    'sacred objects....'

'potent...'

          ''against death by violence'

shell-litered mud

          chitinous

          iridescent

5.

'O in the middle of the ocean...

'a myrtle tree'

barefoot girls

                    dismounted

white coral cliffs

        bearing fronds

        carved ivory

Psamato

    her lucid grace

Euarne

    sweet-figured

the flowing arms and thighs

                Lysianassa

moondust on their breasts

the fluid fingers

        drift anemones

        in green water

dolphin horses

        woven into dance

6.

Damsel's pavan

bold looks askance

in crystal circumstance

each pirouette sedate

a circle calculate

to the peacock's gait

How eloquent you sway

in contrived delay

How limber the trance

of liquid dalliance

O gentle ladies, bring the spring

to every sleeping thing

'And the spirit that stands by the naked man

'In the Book of Moons defend yee!!

7.

Now in the year of death
     Dolphins mounted
Darker darker
downward darker straight as currents
into the caverns of absence the blind Nereids
deep in a flooding of multiform fishes
tangles of plant hung somber and slow
in a relative sky
     Eyes remembering
Aidoneos' dark in the thickening places,
cuttle shell swollen to threat in the doom light
And the crater
      Aides entrance
bellowing
   fire
the great octopus gush of black
Nereids
  caught and tumbled in rolling dark

sea stallions
    frantic curveting

8.
the hour now
the hour
hearing
    croaky voices of the Sibyl
    crying
        eternity
    <u>In the middle of the sea</u>
    <u>a maypole tree'</u>
    <u>'and the naked man out of the sun'</u>
Then came
    into the lighted country
    stopped world
        definition of crystal
<u>glimmering</u>
fish in aspic

    the yellow sponges

        "grow in the vault

    shark conger octopus

           <u>unmoving</u>'

                manta

                like a barn door

vermicular

sea brains

                the red gorgonians

9.

In a glade

one antlered

fire coral

                spire lifting

                --the maypole tree

and Ikarosjnl

the naked man

                eyes open

finger
> pointing to the sky

So find him
> Galateas of the sea

uneasy
> time blind

a consanguinity
> <u>among the primal grasses</u>
> <u>motionless</u>

uneasy
> crossing
> > crossing over him

shadow
> lapsing across his face
> > <u>Who will bring</u>
> > > <u>the white chilton</u>
> > <u>who the gold</u>
> > > <u>laurel crown?</u>

10.

The man

burnt clear

      sun sacrifice

      oblation of water

---no speech

      to formulate this fable

crouching

      with proportioned ceremony

to take him up

      into Elysium

      And he

      springs awakened at the touch

As a taught string plucked

turns

      ten thousand sounds

Iron bells boom

        flowers

        burst from sand

climbing

        among jewel fish

great opening anemones

              gorgonians in fans

all life again

        at the gates of Spring

11.

Bring! Bring!

        The deathless one

    'that at this blisse bringeth'

into the light again!

Agora

I am working on
my agora, my marketplace, ex machina
the worklife of my mind

"When are you going to get a *real* job?"
Thinking *is* a job!
Stories sculpted from my day
tell what I've been doing!

No rhetoric requested
(except for Socrates, he puts it right)
Minefields of words
speak to the person next in line
(how can I talk to someone I do not know?)

family faces, daily snapshots
names I do not know

scraps without scrapbooks

distant cousins known only by the caption.

Whose family do I share in my family?

Where are all of us? by the roadside?

In the rubble? On the field?

Some names stay. Mary at Kent, rising up, still framed.

Who are the people on these pages

torn and stained, documents of our time.

Memory

In limbo, ideas stretch like rubber bands

across a new green meadow.

no sequential thoughts, just a sense of being

lazy in the mind.

This time is different because you've asked

me to inspect a memory slept away many years ago

awakened with a jolt, sharp, here, plain.

Is it important that it's been crowded out, cast away,

no call but now, piqued, it teeters on the cusp, organized for telling?

Hovering over it, timid to the tongue,

I ask for composure; assurance that I'll get it right,

put it out poignant as it was.

Dear Emily

James and T.S. and Ezra Dear Emily
I am a monarch when the fall wind
Drives me south and into the trees
I am strong.
Blue Morpho
This butterfly
    Blue aging
Looking mournfully at the bright blue sky
    There is a deeper blue for older wings
Fluttering more slowly, peacefully thoughtfully
Against a windless day into night.
    Still strong, but light with spirit.

Dear William
The daffodils spring in tune with yellow winds
Your greetings wash over words
A delicate crust for a changing season

We see what you are saying

Your mood is clear resonance.

Dear Sylvia

I know you had to leave

You spoke so desperately

And no one listened

Shut the door with a bang

We hear you now

Midst mixt lives, loves

Beginning again

Endings?

We were classmates and comrades

Too young to understand

Who you were who we were

We are old of mood now

Hugging wisdom and love

Hoping you can hear our care.

Dear Walt
> Stirring the pot of words and courage
> Wars have come; they never end --

You make us understand the living, the dying
the blood.
We understand your heroes;
they are ours too.

Dear Allen
You took Walt to the supermarket
Commoners shelving their anguish
Understanding him
Did they understand you?

Dear James and T.S. and Ezra
Did you talk to Virginia?
Wisdom grew with love and denial
Chess, myths, religion – biblical references
Glorified and clarified

Horror, dishonor, desire.

Frameworks for human behaviors and yours

Wretchedness you had your own issues

Embracing hopes amidst sexual chaos

Saved by storytelling

New mythologies

The world changes

You,-- sisters brothers lovers do not change.

Derek taught us how to love ourselves!

Fly South!

Notes: Leaning on Emily Dickinson, William Wordsworth, Sylvia Plath, Walt Whitman Allen Ginsberg James and T.S. and Ezra, Virginia Woolf and Derek Walcott

List of Paintings

Portrait of Dora Wheeler, 1882–83. William Merritt Chase (American, 1849-1916). Oil on canvas. The Cleveland Museum of Art, Gift of Mrs. Boudinot Keith in memory of Mr. and Mrs. J. H. Wade 1921.1239

View of Bordeaux, from the Quai des Chartrons, 1874. Eugène Boudin (French, 1824-1898). Oil on fabric. The Cleveland Museum of Art, John L. Severance Fund and Gift of Mrs. Dudley S. Blossom, Jr. 1986.73

Dancers, c. 1896. Edgar Degas (French, 1834-1917). Pastel with charcoal on tracing paper mounted on paper and backed with gray board. The Cleveland Museum of Art, Gift of Mr. and Mrs. J. H. Wade 1916.1043

Fifth Avenue, 1919. Childe Hassam (American, 1859-1935). Oil on canvas. The Cleveland Museum of Art, Anonymous Gift 1952.539

Fifth Avenue Nocturne, c. 1895. Childe Hassam (American, 1859-1935). Oil on canvas. The Cleveland Museum of Art, Anonymous Gift 1952.538

Sunny Autumn Day, 1892. George Inness (American, 1825-1894). Oil on canvas. The Cleveland Museum of Art, Anonymous Gift 1956.578

The Red Kerchief, c. 1868–73. Claude Monet (French, 1840-1926). Oil on fabric. The Cleveland Museum of Art, Bequest of Leonard C. Hanna, Jr. 1958.39

Spring Flowers, 1864. Claude Monet (French, 1840-1926). Oil on fabric. The Cleveland Museum of Art, Gift of the Hanna Fund 1953.155

Water Lilies (Agapanthus), c. 1915–26. Claude Monet (French, 1840-1926). Oil on canvas. The Cleveland Museum of Art, John L. Severance Fund and an anonymous gift 1960.81

Bathers Playing with a Crab, c. 1897. Pierre-Auguste Renoir (French, 1841-1919). Oil on fabric. The Cleveland Museum of Art, Purchase from the J. H. Wade Fund 1939.269

Edge of the Woods Near L'Hermitage, Pontoise, 1879. Camille Pissarro (French, 1830-1903). Oil on fabric. The Cleveland Museum of Art, Gift of the Hanna Fund 1951.356

About the Author

Some more context...

   Poetry has been a life venture for Nina.

- At Laurel School. Her first poetry ventures translations from Latin and in English class.

- In the presence of poets her entire life. Including studies with Horace Gregory (Sarah Lawrence College), Louis Zukofsky (San Francisco Poetry Center), Vincent McHugh (San Francisco — Retired chair of Federal Writing Project, NYC), a workshop with Alicia Ostriker, and communication with Naomi Shihab Nye, Robert Pinsky, Alberta Turner. Friend of Richard Howard, Cleveland native Pulitzer Prize MacArthur Award winner — encouraging encounters.

- Read in San Francisco as part of the group working with Vincent McHugh in bars and on the stage as a fore-act to Allen Ginsberg's performance.

- Active with Poet's League of Cleveland.

- Publications: *And So I Must Imagine* (XLibris 2009). Co-editor with Mary Weems and Larry Smith of Cleveland Poetry Scenes: *A Panorama and Anthology* (Bottom Dog Press 2008) Piloted at John Hay High School and Shaker Heights Middle School and Cleveland Public Libraries. *18 Gardens and their Gardeners* with Michael Loderstedt, photographer, 1999 an Ohio Arts Council Art Project Grant.

- Taught creative writing at The Cleveland Museum of Art in East Cleveland arts project.

- Co-Director, *Silver Apples of the Moon* project asking for community response to poetry and art — with Shaker Heights Public Library, Cleveland Public Library, & The Cleveland Museum of Art, & the Cuyahoga County Library. Book edited by Neal Chandler, Cleveland State University.

- Read in museums, bookstores, and libraries in Cleveland.

- Special poetry workshops with the writers and staff of Tupelo Press including Ilya Kaminsky

- Participation in 3 month-long sessions of Tupelo Press 30/30 project with challenge to write a poem a day for each month.

- Review for Tupelo Press of Sean Simon's "Day in a Taxi". 2022

"we are connected underneath the seafloor of our psyches" from *Poetry and Healing: Some Moments of Wholeness* by Alicia Ostriker in the *American Poetry Review*, March/April 2018.

www.ingramcontent.com/pod-product-compliance
Lightning Source LLC
Chambersburg PA
CBHW061802070526
44586CB00023B/2682